# *In The Shadows*

## THE ENSLAVED PEOPLE AND ESTATE WORKERS OF BELMONT MANSION

COMPILED BY

MARK BROWN
EXECUTIVE DIRECTOR, BELMONT MANSION
&
DR. ERICA HAYDEN,
ASSISTANT PROFESSOR, DEPT. OF HISTORY,
TREVECCA UNIVERSITY

PUBLISHED BY
BELMONT MANSION ASSOCIATION
NASHVILLE, TENNESSEE

2018
FOURTH PRINTING

# TABLE OF CONTENTS

PREFACE - 5

BEFORE THE CIVIL WAR – 7

AFTER THE CIVIL WAR – 17

LIST OF ENSLAVED PEOPLE – 20

OTHER SERVANTS
AND ESTATE EMPLOYEES – 37

BOARD OF ASSESSIONS RECORDS – 52

SLAVE SCHEDULE, U. S. CENSUS, 1860 – 62

U. S. AGRICULTURAL CENSUS, 1860 — 63

**FRONT COVER IMAGE**
*EVA SNOWDEN BAKER (1856-1939)*

BY GLADYS WARE LIGON (NASHVILLE, 1892-1987)
PASTEL ON PAPER, PROBABLY FROM A PHOTOGRAPH

2001.05.02 BELMONT MANSION COLLECTION

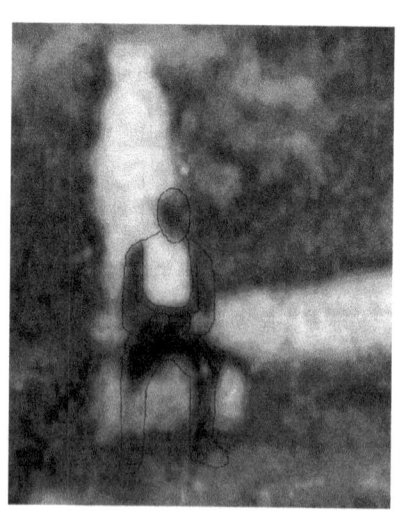

4

# PREFACE

Dated ca. 1860, the landscape painting of the Belmont estate (see page 35) contains elements of an appropriate metaphor for this study, not only of the enslaved people but of all the other people who lived and worked at Belmont before and after the Civil War. These people were usually visible only *in the shadows.* In the painting, an enslaved man is emerging from behind grape vines in the vegetable garden, while the gardener is standing beside the conservatory. Also visible on the periphery of the canvas are two brick slave quarters, a stable, a carriage house, and a gardener's cottage.

The image on the preceding page was taken by a Civil War era photographer in 1864. It depicts the view of Adelicia and Joseph Acklen's estate from the top of the water tower. Several people are shown in the photo, including a nurse standing with Pauline, Adelicia's daughter, and another worker sitting on the base of a statue. These subtle artistic nuances reflect the roles of the workers, both enslaved and hired, who were depicted in keeping with the time period's custom of invisibility.

During the time the family occupied Belmont as a private residence, 8,500 square feet of service area in the ground level basement was accessed by a staircase located in the hall outside the formal dining room. This descent into the basement is yet another metaphor for the invisible position of the people who were crucial to the running of the estate. Unfortunately, there is not a great deal of information about the basement available. The area is not mentioned or referenced in a single family letter or description of the house save one: in his unpublished memoirs, the aide-de-camp to General Thomas J. Wood wrote about using two rooms in the basement for offices of the occupying Union army before the Battle of Nashville.

It is our primary mission at Belmont Mansion to tell the entire story of life at Belmont from the time Adelicia Franklin purchased the property in 1849, until the last family member left in 1886. Our narrative also includes the lives of the people, both enslaved and hired, who worked here at Belmont, as well as at the family's adjoining garden farm called Montvale.

The lists of workers were compiled from several sources, including censuses and city directories. Due to the lack of last names for most of the enslaved people, the task of researching them following their emancipation has proved difficult, if not impossible. There is more information available about the paid employees because their last names were often known. Most importantly, following the Civil War, there was more local news reported in Nashville newspapers providing information about events at Belmont.

This booklet is divided into three sections: an overview of the staff both before and after the Civil War, detailed lists of the enslaved people and hired workers, and transcripts of original documents. While the information seen herein regarding the enslaved residents and the hired staff at Belmont is minimal, we hope this publication will enable other researchers to connect these details with their research. If you have any information on the enslaved population, family stories, papers, or letters about Belmont, we hope you will contact us with that information.

I extend thanks to Dr. Erica Hayden for her work researching this topic and compiling the information into the detailed list of the enslaved and hired workers; Ed Houk for photographing the tombstones of the gardeners; and Grace Mohs and Danielle Ullrich for the graphic design and layout for this publication. I would also like to thank: Virginia Graves for her years of research on all aspects of Belmont Mansion; Dr. Brenda Jackson-Abernathy for her advice; and Bonne Crigger and Deborah Katherine Lovett for editing and proofing this publication.

Mark Brown, Executive Director
Belmont Mansion

# BEFORE THE CIVIL WAR

It is important to recognize there were both enslaved individuals and immigrant servants living and working at Belmont before the Civil War. In order to better understand these people's roles, it is necessary to include a description of the structures and landscapes which they inhabited on a daily basis. Personal details found in primary sources are also presented to help illuminate their contributions to everyday life at Belmont.

Adelicia Hayes Franklin purchased the Belmont property in 1849 before her marriage in May to Joseph Alexander Smith Acklen. At that time, she lived at her Cherry Street residence in downtown Nashville. Construction of the mansion began soon after. According to census records, by October 1850, 13 slaves — 8 males and 5 females ranging in age from 4 months to 30 years — were living on the site.

Set on an approximately 175 acre summer estate, the mansion was built in the Italian villa style and was completed in 1853. In 1857, the art gallery, containing five bedrooms, a bowling alley, and visiting servant quarters in its basement, was built west of the mansion. The mansion was enlarged in 1859 to incorporate the Grand Salon. The water supply for all the structures came from cisterns with pumps; a coal-fired gas plant supplied fuel to light the gasoliers in the mansion. Also on site were a conservatory, a water tower, and zoo grounds.

The 1860 United States Census recorded 32 slaves living at Belmont in ten houses (see page 61). Of that number, 10 were adult males, 10 were adult females, and 12 were children under the age of 15. The oldest female was 45, the oldest male was 30, and the youngest child was one month old.

The north boundary of the estate was approximately where Wedgewood Avenue is located today, the east boundary ran along 12th Avenue South, and the west boundary along 21st Avenue South (see page 29). To the south, a 100-acre garden farm called Montvale was located just beyond Adelicia's conservatory and water tower (known today as the university's bell tower). Behind the water tower was a gardener's brick cottage. The 1860 United States Census listed Leon Geny, age 35, as the gardener. He was born in France and did not speak English. His helper was Robert Kunz, age 22, who was born in Germany.

Residing in the house with the family was the live-in tutor Miss Heloise Cenas. Formerly of New Orleans, Miss Cenas was fluent in the French language. French was actually the second language of Belmont, since Adelicia and the children all spoke it. Also living here was Mrs. Routh, the housekeeper. We believe she was the widow of a plantation owner who lived near Adelicia's West Feliciana Parish property in Louisiana.

Belmont's carriage house and stables were located close to the corner of today's 15th and Acklen Avenues. Next to these structures, the slave dwellings stood in a row leading toward the mansion. The mansion's ground floor basement may have included living space for workers who served mainly in the house.

A property such as Belmont, with its mansion, its grounds and gardens, its animals, and its crops, required a wide variety of workers. First, a general manager or overseer was needed. The Southern Claims Commission records specified that the overseer's house at Montvale was two-stories, brick, and covered with a tin roof. In 1860, the United State Census listed David Henderson (born in Scotland) as the overseer, living there with his wife and four children. The property also contained four or five two-room slave dwellings, each occupied by two families. Three dwellings were brick with tin roofs and one or two were frame structures. All these buildings were torn down in December 1864 in preparation for the Battle of Nashville. The breastworks of the Federal line ran through the overseer's house.

Many of the slaves raised livestock and grew crops at Montvale to provide food and work animals. The 1860 Agriculture Census listed 14 horses, 6 mules, 6 milk cows, 15 cattle, 20 sheep, and 15 pigs (see page 54). The horses were probably stabled at Belmont while the other animals lived at Montvale. Records indicate Adelicia provided the gardener two mules for his use. Poultry was not listed on the census, but Adelicia claimed 150 head of poultry (both chickens and turkeys) were on the property on November 30, 1864. However, by December $15^{th}$ no poultry was left because 3,000 Union troops occupying the area needed provisions. The census also listed the amount of crops grown to feed livestock: 40 tons of hay, 300 bushels of oats, and 500 bushels of corn (some probably also ground for meal). Sheep produced 50 pounds of wool. Food stock for the family and workers consisted of 75 bushels of Irish potatoes, 75 bushels of sweet potatoes, and 350 pounds of butter. Pigs were slaughtered and cured in the smokehouse. There were also orchards, vineyards, and blueberry bushes. Another interesting fact the census included was the value of the Acklen's farm implements, listed at $1,000, which was used to farm 177 acres. Mr. Elliston, a neighbor, also listed $1,000 for farm implements, but he was farming 600 acres.

The household staff duties were patterned after the English servant model. A cook and helpers prepared meals in the ground floor basement. Assisting them was a washerwoman, who cleaned not only pots and pans, but clothing as well.

A butler supervised the laying of fires, the filling of oil lamps, the carrying of food up from the kitchen, and the serving in the dining rooms. To assist him with serving at the table, there may have been two other servants in the dining room, including a woman, and possibly a young man. The butler also managed "At Home" days for Adelicia by answering the door in the Front Hall to receive her guests.

Maids and nurses kept the bedrooms and helped in the nursery. Daily jobs included bringing fresh water for the washstands, emptying the chamber pots, filling the lamps and cleaning their chimneys, airing the bedding, and sweeping out the fireplaces in winter. According to William (Adelicia's second son), Frances was the family nanny. This may have been the same Frances, wife of Brutus, who had been the enslaved personal servant of Adelicia's first husband, Isaac Franklin. Brutus took on the same role for Joseph Acklen until spring 1857. His responsibilities included caring for clothing and guns, mixing drinks, packing/unpacking, and bringing hot water for shaving.

Adelicia required a personal maid who could also serve as a seamstress. The main job of this attendant was to care for clothing and help with dressing and undressing. Housework was carried out by two maids and another man to help with heavy chores.

In addition to the house help, at least one or two coachmen or drivers, possibly one for Adelicia and one for Joseph, were in charge of the stables. A groomsman and stable hand assisted. A young footman, age 9 to 15, attended the coachman.

Enslaved workers brought in coal daily to power the gas plant. Once the coal was turned into gas and refined, a system of underground pipes delivered it to the gasoliers in the mansion. Coal also ran the steam engine that pumped water to the top of the water tower for the irrigation system and the fountains. Other workers cared for the animals in the zoo.

Some of the enslaved were required to travel with the family. There are records indicating the children's nurse, the tutor, and the housekeeper traveled with the family to the Angola plantation in Louisiana, or were sent ahead with the trunks.

## *THE ENSLAVED AT BELMONT*

Understanding the everyday life of enslaved African Americans at Belmont from a 21st century perspective is fraught with many pitfalls. Written records are few and visual records, with the exception of one image, are non-existent. Unlike many Southern ladies of the time, such as the prolific Mary Chestnut of South Carolina, Adelicia Acklen was no antebellum diarist. We only know of seventy odd letters she wrote to various relatives and friends. In those letters, Adelicia never recorded any personal opinions about slavery or about the people who worked for her. However, we do have a letter from her second husband, Joseph Acklen, which gives a great deal of insight into his thinking. At present, there are no known firsthand accounts of the enslaved people who lived and worked at Belmont.

A few sentences in Adelicia's letters to family members give us a glimpse into the lives of the family and those who took care of everyday tasks — *"Frances is taking care of the baby,"* and *"Have Joe help Mary put up the lace curtains before we get back from Louisiana."* Also, legal documents, such as censuses, inventories, and lawsuits, do shed light on who lived, and what was found, on the property. Finally, at the beginning of the 20th century, Adelicia's middle son William wrote his memoirs, *Scion of Belmont*. His reflections are from the viewpoint of a romantic looking back on a privileged childhood, but he does provide information about life at Belmont. (*Tennessee Historical Quarterly, Vol. XXXVIII, No. 1* and *No. 2, Spring & Summer,* edited by John Kiser)

What do these primary sources say about day-to-day life at Belmont during that period from late summer 1853 when the Acklens moved into Belmont until December 15, 1864, when the Battle of Nashville commenced? How many slaves lived at Belmont and what did they do? Most importantly, do we know who they were?

The first question to pose is, how many enslaved people lived on the properties Adelicia owned? Her first husband, Isaac Franklin, was a former slave trader. Upon her marriage to him in 1839, her father O. B. Hayes gave her Betsy and Maria, two adult slave women who had five and two children respectively. Isaac Franklin died in 1846 leaving behind 716 enslaved people. 137 lived on his farm called Fairvue in Sumner County near Gallatin, Tennessee. The other 579 lived at his cotton-producing plantations in West Feliciana Parish, Louisiana. Of these numbers, we do not know how many worked in the house or in the fields. At his death, he left Adelicia an unknown number of household slaves from Fairvue. The remaining people were assigned to work at the Isaac Franklin Institute. The Institute was intended to be a school endowed by Franklin's estate, but it never opened; subsequently, those slaves were sold. Some of the formerly enslaved workers at Fairvue remained with Adelicia at Belmont until she moved to Washington, D.C., in 1884.

The 1860 United States Census listed 659 slaves in Louisiana, making Adelicia the third largest slaveholder in Louisiana and the seventh largest slaveholder in the United States.

## *ENSLAVED CONDITIONS*

In 1860, there were 48 people living on the Belmont estate including the Acklens, the tutor, the housekeeper, the gardeners, and the overseer with his family. The number of slaves — 10 adult men, 10 adult women, and 8 children under the age of ten — implies the probability of family units. By the building standards of the day, brick and frame structures with tin roofs were considered adequate protection from the elements.

Without archaeological investigation, it is difficult to determine foodways. The 1860 Agricultural Census provided some information about what was grown and raised at Belmont, such as Irish and sweet potatoes. Corn in the form of corn meal was a staple in the diet. Hogs and cattle were slaughtered, with the lesser cuts of meat given to the enslaved. In 1856 and 1857, the well-circulated southern magazine *Debow's Review* (Vol. XXI, pages 617-620 and Vol. XXII, pages 376-381) published an article written by Joseph Acklen called *Rules for the Management of a Southern Estate*. In the article, also distributed as a pamphlet, Acklen stated slaves should be given fresh meat occasionally, as opposed to cured meat. He also felt there should be sufficient milk cows to provide milk for all the slaves.

Assuming Belmont was operated in a similar fashion to the plantations in Louisiana, there were stated hours for breakfast and dinner. Dinner consisted of properly prepared vegetables, meat, and bread. No ardent spirits were permitted. Enslaved people were not allowed to raise any kind of livestock.

On the Acklen plantations in Louisiana, "an intelligent and otherwise suitable woman will be appointed as a nurse upon each plantation, who will administer medicine and otherwise attend upon the sick." (*DeBow's Review*, Vol. XXII, page 377). In his memoirs *Scion of Belmont*, William recalled the nurses were "older women." The slaves would also receive medical care from a physician. In Louisiana, the doctor who treated Isaac Franklin at his death was the same doctor who treated the enslaved workers. A dentist also visited annually. However, according to family folklore, the slaves did not look on this as a benefit.

Sundays were a day of visiting and rest. Enslaved workers were expected to be up, dressed in clean clothes, and have their quarters orderly. On the plantations in Louisiana, Joseph provided preachers only of his choosing and allowed no meetings beyond ten o'clock at night.

As for punishment, the only record available is from *Rules in the Management of a Southern Estate*, Joseph's 1857 pamphlet. Joseph wrote:

> Whipping is the only punishment that will be permitted, except keeping the disobedient on their plantations. Whipping must never be cruel or severe.... I object to having the skin cut, or my Negroes marked in any way by the lash; and with proper care, this can always be avoided. I will most certainly discharge any overseer for striking any of my Negroes with a club or the butt of his whip or in any way injuring one of my Negroes.... They must be kept under strict discipline, which can be accomplished by talking to them, and punishing moderately, but promptly and certainly.

Joseph reiterated later in the pamphlet that it is "certainty, more than the severity of punishment, that prevents crime." He even stated that any slave could come to him or his agent about problems with the overseer without fear of punishment. There are no other references to any form of punishment from first-hand accounts.

As to how the slaves felt about their treatment from the Acklens, there are no known sources or records available. We do know few of the enslaved could read or write.

## *WERE THE SLAVES AT BELMONT SOLD?*

We have only one account of the family selling a slave. Adelicia wrote to her sister from the Angola plantation in Louisiana on April 29, 1857, that Brutus had been sold because he had "been behaving very badly and drinking all winter." Adelicia inherited Brutus from Isaac Franklin. We do not know if his wife Frances was the same Frances who cared for the children and had a close relationship with Adelicia's son William.

## HOW DID THE ACKLENS FEEL ABOUT SLAVERY?

Both Joseph and Adelicia were acutely aware that they were being watched in their treatment of the enslaved. Northern visitors often inspected their plantations. William wrote in *Scion of Belmont* that during these visits his father intended on "showing the better side of slavery in an ideal plantation life." One such occasion took place in February 1858. Adelicia wrote from Angola in Louisiana that "Several Englishmen among others Mr. Borsing of the great house of Borsing Bro.'s London... are coming up here with some New Yorkers to see for themselves how the Negroes are treated." She adds, "We intend to show them around."

Adelicia grew up in a household with a father who was originally from New England. He did not own any enslaved people until after he moved to Nashville in 1808. In 1852, Adelicia's brother Oliver went on a trip to visit relatives in Massachusetts. Before he left, Mr. Hayes warned his son in a letter, "You will find New England natives quite different from us. Let them enjoy their opinions uncontradicted and especially on the subject of slavery." (*McGavock Hayes Papers*, Tennessee State Library and Archives)

Two weeks before his death in 1863, Joseph wrote to Adelicia from Angola in Louisiana, "...the south has no chance of winning this war and we shall soon be done with this Negro business and I shall be glad of it. I never had much taste for it as you know. I have suffered much from it."

Another account, taken from Elvira J. Powers's *Hospital pencilings: Being a diary while in Jefferson General Hospital, Jeffersonville, Ind., and others at Nashville, Tennessee as a matron and visitor*, revealed the following:

> An intelligent chattel, who has been on the place twenty years, informs us that Achlen was a kind master . . . That when he visited his plantation in Louisiana, the negroes would welcome him at the wharf, and if it was the least muddy, would take him upon their shoulders and carry him to the house. But despite this fact, the negroes have somehow got the impression that freedom is preferable to slavery. So strongly are they impressed with the desire of owning themselves, that out of 900 who were on the estate and plantations at the commencement of the war, but five remain at the former place, and these with wages of $15.00 per week, while about the same number are at each of the plantations, these kept also by wages.
>
> The death of Achlen occurred last fall; his widow is much of the time in New Orleans, but the property is mostly kept by what was formerly a part of itself.

# AFTER THE CIVIL WAR*

After the Civil War, some emancipated individuals continued to live and work at Belmont alongside the immigrants who had previously worked there. The staff reflected the patterns for domestic help common all over the country. Employees were a mixture of African Americans, American-born Caucasians and immigrants from Europe: 36% European-born, 21% American-born, 21% percent African Americans, and 15% unknown, but probably African American.

In the nineteen-year period from 1865 to 1884, the names of 33 servants are known. Using the 1870 and 1880 United States Census, along with other documents, the ethnic makeup of the staff was as follows:

7 African Americans
7 American-born Caucasians
5 unknown, probably African American
3 Swiss
2 Irish
2 Germans
2 French
2 Caucasians, place of birth unknown
1 Scottish
1 English

This somewhat reflects the general immigration patterns for this period. Both German and Irish workers were represented on the Belmont estate. Beginning in the 1840s, Irish swelled the rolls of American immigration records, making them the largest group to immigrate. Second were the Germans, escaping the poverty of their homeland. The number of French employees at Belmont, as well as those of Swiss descent, was disproportionately high when compared to general immigration patterns.

When examining the 1870 and 1880 Davidson County census records, the Irish made up 47.56% and 42.13% of the foreign born population, respectively. The total foreign born population had grown from 4,382 in 1860 to 4,420 in 1870 and dropped slightly by 1880. Germans made up 23.33% in 1870 and 22.79% in 1880. The third largest group immigrated from England and Wales, 9.71% in 1870 and 10.80% in 1880. The fourth largest group, from Switzerland, saw a rise in not only percentage but also in raw numbers between 1870 and 1880. Swiss made up 3.42% (151) in 1870 and 4.90% (203) in 1880. There were 145 (3.28%) Scots living in Davidson County in 1870 and 144 (3.47%) in 1880. The lowest numbers were from France with 128 (2.90%) in 1870 and 90 in 1880 (2.17%). (Census data is taken from *Historical Census Browser*, University of Virginia. <mapserver.lib.virginia.edu/index.html>)

Nashville's immigrant patterns seem consistent with other major cities at the time including New Orleans, New York, and Charleston. "In 1850 Louisiana had the largest concentration of immigrants in the South, about 75,000 people and approximately one-quarter of Louisiana's free population. New Orleans, the largest port in the South and second largest in the nation after New York, was a natural point of entry for people from other countries. Between 1820 and 1860, over half a million immigrants arrived in Louisiana." (Bankston, Carl L. "New People in the South: an Overview of Southern Immigration," *South Cultures* vol. 13, no. 4 [2007]. *US History Collection.*)

Living quarters for Belmont's staff were not documented with the exception of gardeners and live-in tutors. Gardeners and their assistants continued to live in the gardener's cottage; tutors continued living in the house with the family.

Five former slave quarters, all lining the service drive, survived the Civil War. African American employees continued to occupy these brick duplexes. It is possible some of the English-style basement (almost 8,500 square foot) was also used for living quarters.

There is no definitive record of how many former slaves opted to remain in service at Belmont after emancipation or what their names were. We have documentation for only three individuals, but there is no record of how long their service lasted. The 1870 Federal Census listed a Mary Fleming living and working at Belmont. Evidence suggests she may have been a former slave named Mary Ann. Mary Ann's mother was Maria, who Adelicia received from her father upon her marriage to Isaac Franklin in 1839. In a letter written in October 1868, Adelicia mentioned her cook Amanda. This may be the same Amanda who was Betsy's daughter, both of whom Adelicia received from her father in 1839. In April 1869, Adelicia wrote of having hired a new cook. William Acklen, a former slave of the Acklens, testified in court for Adelicia against the Federal government. Adelicia was seeking reparations for damages incurred during the war. The transcript of the trial stated that at the time of his testimony, William was an employee at the estate (see Copy of Records, p. 48).

This scant bit of documentation is all that has survived about the people who worked at Belmont for Adelicia in the two decades following the Civil War. However, what little we have does hold tantalizing clues to individual lives forever altered by the Civil War. Without the assistance of these workers, both African Americans and European immigrants, Adelicia may well have been unable to maintain her lifestyle and sold Belmont out of the family long before the 1880s.

*Census research for this section was done by Lidia Michel and Alysa Yates presented in a paper for a research and writing class for Dr. Erica Hayden at Trevecca University, Nashville, Tennessee.

# LIST OF ENSLAVED PEOPLE BY FAMILY GROUP

Compiled by Erica Hayden, Ph.D.

***Betsy and Children***

<u>Betsy</u>: House slave given to Adelicia by her father O.B. Hayes in 1839. Listed in September 1847 inventory of Isaac Franklin's estate. Listed in May 1849 Joseph Acklen marriage contract as belonging to Adelicia. Listed in October 1857 legal document. Mother of Harriet, James, Alexander, Joseph, Amanda, and Ive.

<u>Alexander</u>: Son of Betsy. Given to Adelicia by her father O. B. Hayes in 1839. Listed in September 1847 inventory of Isaac Franklin's estate. Listed in May 1849 Joseph Acklen marriage contract as belonging to Adelicia. Listed in October 1857 legal document. Sibling of Harriet, James (could be James Alexander), Joe/Joseph, Ive, and Amanda.

<u>Amanda</u>: Daughter of Betsy. Given to Adelicia by her father O. B. Hayes in 1839. Listed in September 1847 inventory of Isaac Franklin's estate. Listed in May 1849 Joseph Acklen marriage contract as belonging to Adelicia. Listed in October 1857 legal document. Sibling of Harriet, James, Alexander, Joe/Joseph, and Ive. Possibly the same Amanda (with no last name given) buried in the Nashville City Cemetery on March 10, 1871.

Most likely, she was the cook referenced in an October 1868 letter from Adelicia By April 1869, Adelicia had a new cook.

<u>Harriet</u>: Daughter of Betsy. Given to Adelicia by her father O.B. Hayes in 1839. Listed in September 1847 inventory of Isaac Franklin's estate. Listed in May 1849

Joseph Acklen marriage contract as belonging to Adelicia. Listed in October 1857 legal document. Sibling of James, Alexander, Joe/Joseph, Ive, and Amanda.

Ive: Daughter of Betsy. Born after September 1847 but before May 1849. Listed in May 1849 Joseph Acklen marriage contract as belonging to Adelicia. Listed in October 1857 legal document. Sibling of Harriet, James, Alexander, Joe/Joseph, and Amanda.

James: Son of Betsy. Possibly known as James Alexander. Given to Adelicia by her father O.B. Hayes in 1839. Listed in September 1847 inventory of Isaac Franklin's estate. Listed in May 1849 Joseph Acklen marriage contract as belonging to Adelicia. Listed in October 1857 legal document. Sibling of Harriet, Alexander, Joe/Joseph, Ive, and Amanda.

Joseph: Son of Betsy. Given to Adelicia by her father O.B. Hayes in 1839. Listed in September 1847 inventory of Isaac Franklin's estate. Listed in May 1849 Joseph Acklen marriage contract as belonging to Adelicia. Listed in October 1857 legal document. Sibling of Harriet, James, Alexander, Ive, and Amanda.

In 1860, Adelicia wrote that Joe was to help Mary put up lace curtains at Belmont. In November 1856, a man named Joe was supposed to wash the flowerpots after Mr. McGrady emptied them; he might be the same Joe/Joseph. In the 1880 and 1881 Nashville City Directories, a Joseph Acklen was listed as African American, working as a laborer at 121 N. Cherry Street. In 1880, his home address was N. Spruce near Gay, and in 1881, Quarry near Line. The 1881 directory listed another Joseph Acklen as African American, also working as a laborer at the Union Stockyard, with a residence on Clinton near Walnut.

## *Baker and Snowden Families*

Baker, John:   Born ca. 1820. Slave at Fairvue. According to records dated September 28, 1847, he was 27 years old at the time. Married to Betsy or Bettie Baker.

> Baker, Betsy or Bettie: Born ca. 1825 at Mount Vernon, Virginia. Purchased by Isaac Franklin from John Washington, adopted son of George Washington. Slave at Fairvue, according to records dated September 28, 1847, and listed as being 20 years old at the time. Married to John Baker. Listed as having at least 9 children. The 1910 census noted 15 children with 6 still alive. Died in 1923 at Peach Valley in Sumner County, Tennessee.
>
> Ruffin Baker, one of her sons, born ca. 1846, has more information on Betsy/Bettie listed under his own entry below. Besides Ruffin, according to some records, Betsy/Bettie also had a son Mark Baker, born in 1847 or 1853. He married Fannie who lived from 1861 to before 1900. Betsy/Bettie also had a daughter, Hanna Baker, born in February 1858. Mark and Hanna are easily traceable because Betsy/Bettie lived with her adult children near the end of her life. The 1900 census listed Hanna (age 42) as head of household, living with her brother Mark (age 53), nephews Willie (age 22), Mark (age 18), and another nephew whose name is illegible (age 15), and her mother Betsy/Bettie (age 80). In the 1910 census, Mark (age 56), Hanna (age 53), and Betsy/Bettie (age 90), were all residing together. In the 1920 census, Mark (age 68), lived with Hanna (age 64), and Betsy/Bettie (age 107, but more   likely 101). It is noted Mark and Hanna could read and write; Betsy/Bettie could not read or write. The age discrepancies are within a logical margin of error for census records.
>
> Ruffin:   Most likely the son of Bettie/Betsy and John Baker. Listed as  two years old on a September 28, 1847,

inventory. Born ca. 1846; married Mary Jane Sergeant (born 1850) on April 23, 1870. They had the following children: John (born 1869), Celina (born April 1882), Alex (born October 1892), and Anna May (born June 1893). Two grandchildren were also listed in the record: Brutus (born September 1892) and Margaret or Martha Ann (born August 1889). There was a Mark Baker who was likely the son of Ruffin (not listed in the notes above), born in April 1875, and married in 1895 to Hannah, also born in April 1875. According to the 1910 census, Mark and Hannah, both age 34, lived with their children, Henry, age 14 (born May 1896), Anthony, age 11 (born June 1899), Parker, age 8, Jennie, age 6, and another son, Dorsey, age 3.

Aggie: According to family tradition, Aggie was the personal maid to Adelicia and sometimes took care of the children. She traveled with the family to New York in 1866. While there, she met and married Sam. Aggie remained in New York until Sam's death and then moved back to Fairvue. It is believed she was the mother of Eva Snowden Baker (the cover image on this publication).

Baker, Eva Snowden: Born ca. 1856, and died in 1939. (Portrait on front cover). According to family tradition, she was Adelicia's personal maid or personal dresser after the Civil War. It appears she married three times. We believe her maiden name to be Snowden, but it is possible her first marriage was to a Snowden, then perhaps to a Lane and finally to a Baker, according to her children's surnames. One of her marriages was to Mark Baker (b. ?, d. 1940). He was one of Betsy Baker's nine children. Betsy was born in 1825 at Mount Vernon in Virginia and died in Sumner County. (The 1870 census for Sumner County listed an Eva, age 12, daughter of Richard Dixon, age 28, and his wife Hannah, age 22, and sister, Dinah, age 3. This family is only a possible match for Eva Snowden Baker.)

The 1900 census listed her as Eva Snowden, age 45, having eight children and being head of the household. At least five of her children were by Mark Baker. In 1900, she lived with Peter Snowden, age 23 (born March 1877); Neal or Sarah Lane, age 17 (born May 1883, although some records say 1893); Gus Lane, age 13, (born August 1886 or 1889); Baby Love Baker, age 8 (born June 1891); Eldritch or Eldridge Baker, age 6 (born November 1894); Ruffin Baker, age 3, (born November 22, 1895 or 1896); and Bennie Baker, age 6 months (born November 1899). In 1900, she was living in the Peach Valley area of Sumner County with a number of other former slaves from Fairvue. She cannot be found in the 1910 census. In 1920, the Sumner County census listed her as 61 years old and living with Ben, age 40; an illegible male name, age 38; Wilkins, age 34; and Gertrude, age 30. The 1930 census listed her living in Peach Valley with her sister Sally Ann Smith, a widow. Eva is listed as being able to read and write.

## *Brutus and Fanny*

Brutus: Isaac Franklin's valet. Married to Fanny/Frances. Given to Adelicia by Isaac in his 1846 will. Sent to Louisiana (Angola Plantation) in September 1847 as he may have been involved in or sympathetic to the attempted murder of the overseer at Fairvue. Following Adelicia's marriage to Joseph Acklen, he became Joseph's valet. On April 29, 1857, Adelicia wrote that he was sold in New Orleans from Angola Plantation for "drinking all winter and behaving very badly." He was jailed on several occasions. Purchased by a General Pike and taken to Little Rock, Arkansas. Died on December 22, 1869, having by this time taken the last name of Jackson. A newspaper wrote a story about him and recounted his recovery from heavy drinking.

Fanny/Frances: Wife of Brutus. House servant given to Adelicia by Isaac Franklin in his will. It is still unclear if this is the same Frances who was the children's nurse. (See separate entry below.)

## *Maria and Children*

Maria: House slave given to Adelicia by her father O.B. Hayes in 1839. Listed in September 1847 inventory of Isaac Franklin's estate. Listed in May 1849 Joseph Acklen marriage contract as belonging to Adelicia. Listed in October 1857 legal document. Mother of Ezekiel, William, and Mary Ann.

> Ezekiel or Zeke: Son of Maria. Given to Adelicia by her father O.B. Hayes, in 1839. Listed in September 1847 inventory of Isaac Franklin's estate. Listed in May 1849 marriage contract as belonging to Adelicia. Sibling of William and Mary Ann.
>
> Mary Ann: Daughter of Maria. Given to Adelicia by her father O.B. Hayes in 1839. Listed in 1847 inventory of Isaac Franklin's estate. Listed in May 1849 Joseph Acklen marriage contract as belonging to Adelicia. Listed in October 1857 legal document. Sibling of Ezekiel and William.

In 1860, Adelicia wrote that Mary, with the help of Joe, was to put up lace curtains at Belmont. She was to regulate the house as well. Mary Ann could be Mary Fleming, an African American servant listed as working at Belmont in the 1870 census, 28 years old and born in Tennessee. Her actual age would be 31 in 1870 if she were a year old or less in 1839. The difference of 3 years is within the range of age discrepancies found in census records. For more information on Mary Fleming, see her listing under the "Other Servants and Estate Workers" section.

William Acklen: Born between September 1847 and May 1849. Son of Maria, who was given to Adelicia by her father O.B. Hayes in 1839. While not listed on the 1847 inventory of Isaac Franklin's estate, he is listed in the May 1849 Joseph Acklen marriage contract as belonging to Adelicia.

In 1866, a William Acklen, age 19, a former slave of Adelicia's and a servant after the war, was called as a witness for damages that occurred at Belmont during the Civil War. This document indicated his birth year as 1847. An 1857 legal document listing slaves given to Adelicia by O.B. Hayes noted Maria, along with her children Ezekiel and Mary Ann, and then William. This name order may indicate William was likely born after 1847.

Other Known Listings For William Acklen
It is difficult to know whether any of the following men are the same William Acklen who lived at Belmont, but they are included here for reference.

William Acklen or William Acker: Married Rosa Powers by Reverend Lemon on September 28, 1865, in Davidson County. (Book 5, page 75)

William A. Acklen: Married Mary A. Boyd on April 4, 1889, by J.M. Mitchell in Davidson County. (Book 9, page 155)

The 1890 Nashville City Directory listed a William Acklen living on Deluge Street. This person is not listed in the 1889 or 1891 directory. A William (Billy) Acklen died July 31, 1890, age 70. He was born in Tennessee, married, and resided on Deluge Street. He died of dysentery, and his death was certified by Dr. Richard Cheatham (son of Adelicia's third husband Dr. William A. Cheatham). He was buried at Mt. Ararat Cemetery. This is probably not the same William Acklen as this man would have been born around 1820; the William in most of Belmont's records would have been born ca. 1847. A Mary Acklen, widow of William, lived at 819 High Street in 1896.

William Acklen: The 1889 and 1890 Nashville City Directories listed William R. Acklen as a driver. By 1893, he was listed as a salesman. Listed as a painter in the City Directories of 1900, 1902, 1903, 1909, and 1913.

William D. Acklen: Listed in the 1900 directory as a porter.

## *Individual Slaves*

Frances: Probably the same Frances who was the children's nurse. Mentioned in letter dated December 1857, as taking care of the baby. Mentioned in a letter from Adelicia in April 1860.

Gant (aka Grant), Ben: Born ca. 1831. Listed on the estate inventory at Fairvue on September 28, 1847. In 1848, Adelicia "hired" him, and he was still with her in September of 1854. By March of 1861, he was "attached" to the Angola Plantation and was married to Maria Gant (Grant) who was born ca. 1841. They had a son, also named Ben. (Vertical Record at the Sumner County Archives, Mortgage Statement, March 15, 1861 in New Orleans.)

Georgiana: Given to Adelicia by Isaac Franklin in his will.

Gibbs, Rena: Born ca. 1833. Listed on the estate inventory at Fairvue on September 28, 1847, where she was part of the house staff. Her mother was Maria Gibbs, born ca. 1815. By September 1847, Rena had two younger sisters, Louisiana, born ca. 1838, and Rachael, born ca. 1841. She also had a brother, Martin, born ca. 1845.

She was "hired" by Adelicia in 1848 from the Trustees of the Franklin Institute. By September of 1854, she had two children, names unknown. In November of 1857, she was mentioned in a letter as being at Belmont after the Acklens had left for Louisiana. (Vertical Record at the Sumner County Archives.)

London: Buried at Old City Cemetery on February 16, 1850, on the Poplar lot, at the cost of $2.00. Listed as slave of J.A.S. Acklen at the time of death; age and cause of death unrecorded. Lived at Adelicia's house on Cherry Street. (*Nashville City Cemetery Records* [5-1862: *133*]. Found online at the Nashville Public Library website.)

Marcius: Given to Adelicia by Isaac Franklin in his will.

Mortimer: Listed in May 1849 Joseph Acklen marriage contract as belonging to Adelicia. There is no record of him before or after this document.

Randolph: Slave impressed by the Federal Army to build Fort Negley in 1862. (*Employment Rolls and Nonpayment Rolls of Negroes Employed in the Defenses of Nashville, Tennessee, 1862-1863*. File #98, Tennessee State Library and Archives.)

Salley: Listed as "servant to Cpl. Joseph A.S. Acklim" [sic] when buried at the Old City Cemetery on March 21, 1862, in the "Negro lot" at the cost of $4.00; age 23 and died of "Pneumonie." (*Nashville City Cemetery records (5-1862:133)*. Found online at the Nashville Public Library website.)

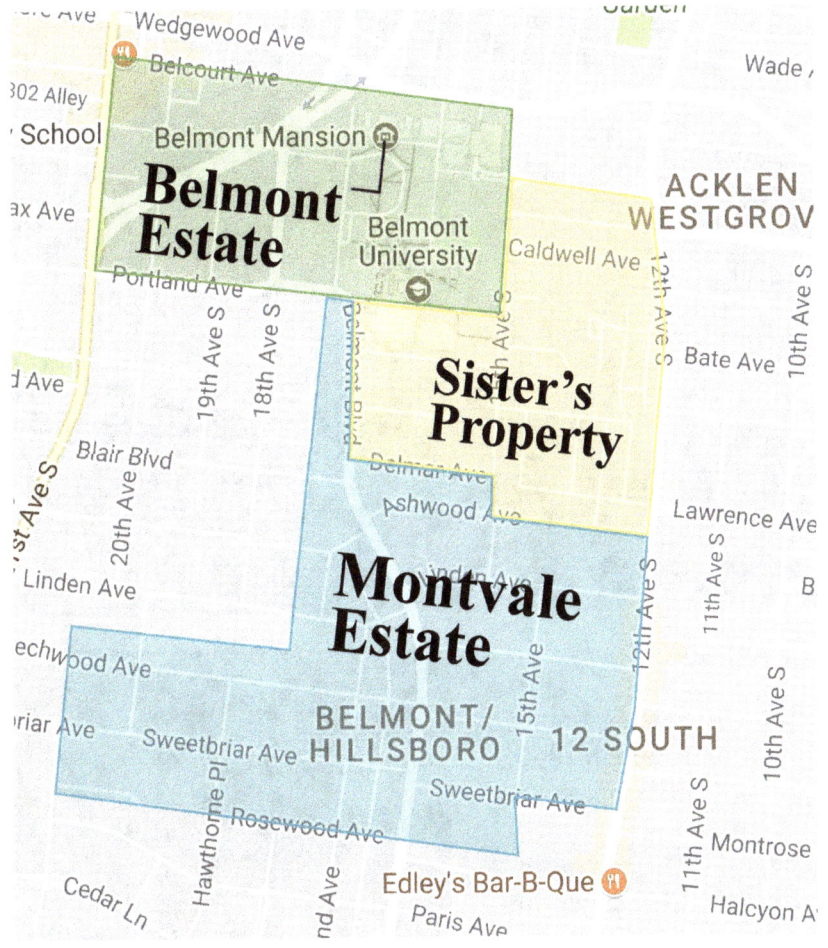

**Map of Belmont/Hillsboro Neighborhood**

Modern map of the neighborhood around Belmont Mansion includes an approximate overlay of the property owned by Adelicia, as well as her sister's (Corrine Lawrence) adjoining property.

**Top:** Belmont Estate painting completed in 1860, artist unknown.

**Middle:** Possible stables in background of Belmont Estate painting.

**Bottom:** Carriage driver in Belmont Estate painting.

**Bottom:**
Unidentified enslaved man emerging from the grape vines in the Belmont Estate painting.

**Top:**
Slave quarters behind the bath house from the Belmont Estate painting.

**Bottom:**
Photograph of slave quarters at Fairvue in Sumner County, Tennessee. Presumably the quarters at Belmont looked similar to these structures. (Image courtesy of the Tennessee State Library and Archives).

**Top Left:**
Belmont estate slave quarters hidden in the trees in the Belmont Estate painting.

**Bottom Left and Right:**
Modern gravestones erected in 2016 for two of Adelicia's enslaved workers, London and Salley.

**Top:** Gardener's cottage from the Belmont Estate painting.

**Left Middle:** Headstone for Leon Geny, gardener at Belmont.

**Right Side:** Gardener beside the conservatory from the Belmont Estate painting.

**Left Side:**
Headstone for Valentine Fischer, gardener at Belmont.

**Right Middle:**
Details on Henry Gray's headstone.

**Bottom:**
Headstone for Henry Gray, gardener at Belmont. The Acklen mausoleum is in the background.

**Heloise Cenas 1837-1911 - Tutor**
Artist Unknown
Image Courtesy of Louisiana State Museum

# OTHER SERVANTS AND ESTATE EMPLOYEES ACCORDING TO STARTING DATE OF EMPLOYMENT/FIRST OCCURRENCE IN RECORDS

Complied by Erica Hayden, Ph.D.

## *1850s*

Routh, Mrs.: It is believed she worked as a housekeeper. There was an advertisement for a housekeeper in December 1855. Two applications were received, one from Mrs. Routh and another from the housekeeper of Adelicia's friend, Mrs. James K. Polk. Mrs. Routh was mentioned in two of Adelicia's letters:
December 20, 1855 letter — Rode with Adelicia.
November 1857 letter — Wanted her workbox sent down to Louisiana; it was on the mantel in the housekeeper's room. She also wanted her riding hat, which was upstairs in the wardrobe.

McGrady, Mr.: Mentioned in an 1856 letter that he was to empty the flowerpots. He was no longer at Belmont by April 1860. Most likely, this was D. A. McGrady (D. may stand for David). He exhibited at the Horticultural Society Exhibition in May 1868, and at the Agricultural and Mechanical Association Fair in October 1872. He was a partner with Gartland.

Bonstead, Mr.: In December 1857, Adelicia wrote in a letter that he was to clean out the cistern for drinking water and examine the corner of the nursery for leaks. In February 1858, she wrote again about the cistern.

# *1860s*

<u>Geny, Leon</u>: Born ca. 1826 in France. Geny family tradition indicated that in 1858, Leon and his brother John Geny arrived in Nashville from Alsace, France, to design Belmont's gardens. It is more likely Leon Geny became the gardener upon, or soon after, his arrival and that the gardens had already been designed. However, he may have made changes to the original designs. An April 1860 letter indicated he was at Belmont working as the gardener. The June 1860 census listed Geny as age 35 and living in the gardener's house with Robert Kunze. According to Nashville newspapers, we know the following information: in December 1864, he was no longer the gardener at Belmont; in 1868 he was elected to the Tennessee Horticultural Society; in September 1869 he was working for Mr. P. I. Nichols.

Geny was not listed in the 1870 census. He became the gardener at Belmont again in September 1873, and worked for one year. He became a U.S. citizen on July 25, 1871. He was married to Annie L. (sometimes spelled Anna) who was born 1830 in Metz of the province of Loraine, France. In April 1874, he and his wife bought five acres on Hillsboro Pike near Belmont for $2,500 where they grew plants and flowers to sell at the farmers' market in Nashville. Leon died on January 24, 1878, and was buried at Mount Olivet Cemetery with Masonic rites from Cumberland Lodge, No. 8 of which he was a member. They had one son Jacob (1857-1907) who continued growing vegetables and flowers after his mother's death in 1893.

The 1879 and 1880 City Directory listed a Leon Geny as a gardener. The directories from 1892 onward listed him as a florist. This was a nephew, the son of John B. Geny, who in 1868 started a florist business in Nashville that is still in the family today.

<u>Henderson, David</u>: Listed in the 1860 census, age 35. Born in Scotland. He was the overseer at Montvale, and lived in

overseer's house with his wife Jennett, age 35, and four children: Mary, age 10, George, age 9, Harriett, age 6, and Andrew, 6 months. It appears Andrew was the first child born in Tennessee.

David was no longer at Belmont by December 1862. There was a David Henderson listed in the 1865 and 1866 city directories who owned a livery stable on North Cherry and lived at 108 North Cherry. This does not appear to be the same person. He was not identified in other censuses.

Kunze, Robert: Listed in the 1860 census, age 22. Born in Germany, and living with Leon Geny in the gardener's cottage at Belmont.

The 1870 census listed a Robert Kunze, age 30, from Prussia. He worked as a farm laborer in Austin County, Texas, and was living with Peter Pampel, 24, and Bertha Pampel, 20. Bertha was from Prussia, and Peter was from Texas.

The 1880 Austin County Census listed a Robert Kunze, age 39. He worked as a farmer, with wife Mathilda, age 25, who kept house and was born in Texas. Three children lived with the couple: Willie, age 8; Frank, age 6; and Edward, age 3.

The 1920 census listed Robert as still living in Austin County, age 81, with Matilda, age 61. It was recorded he immigrated in 1853, naturalized in 1860, and owned his own house. Both he and his wife could read and write.

He was buried at San Felipe de Austin Cemetery in San Felipe, Texas. According to his grave stone, he was born on March 29, 1839, and lived until December 24, 1924. (Find A Grave Memorial # 4426837)

Terry, James C.: The 1850 census indicated he was living in Williamson County, Tennessee. Born around 1819 in Tennessee, he was age 31, a farmer, living with his wife,

Margaret, age 28, and their children: Mary J., age 7; Rufus, age 5; and Rachael, age 1.

The 1860 census for Davidson County listed James, 42, an overseer, living close to Belmont with Margaret, 38, and seven children: Mary, age 17; Rufus, age 15; Rachael, age 11; Charles, age 9; James, age 7; Alice, age 3; and Samuel, 5 months.

Near the end of 1862, James, began working as Adelicia's overseer. He was living in the Overseer's house when it was destroyed during the Battle of Nashville in December 1864.

The 1870 census for Davidson County listed James, 50, working as a lime burner and living with his son Rufus, age 24, head of the household and a farmer. Also living with them were Margaret, age 47; Charles, age 18; James, age 13; Nannie, age 12; Alice, age 10; Samuel, age 8; and Archibald, age 6.

The 1880 census for Davidson County listed James, age 62, as farming. He lived with Margaret, age 60; Charley, age 27, a drover; Nannie, age 21; and Samuel, age 20, also a farmer. Listed as well was Mattie Frazier, granddaughter, age 8. James cannot be located beyond 1880.

Cenas, Heloise: (1837-1911) (Portrait on page 36) Arrived at Belmont from New Orleans with Adelicia in June 1864. We are unsure when she started working as a tutor. In a letter dated September 1864, Miss Cenas wrote to her family in New Orleans that the "grounds are more beautiful than ever." It is assumed she left her position as tutor when Adelicia and the children traveled to Europe in May 1865. She carried on a lifelong correspondence with the children, but was never mentioned again as a tutor at Belmont. Replaced as tutor by Miss Ella Mason.

Miss Cenas was the daughter of Margaret Pierce and Hilary Breton Cenas of New Orleans. Margaret Cenas and her daughters founded the Cenas Institute for girls in 1865 at the corner of Claiborne and Esplanade Avenues. This school continued into the 20th century.

Miss Cenas was educated in Boston (*Memories of a Southern Woman of Letters* by Grace King pp 89-91), and moved to Baltimore to teach. She died in Arlington, Maryland, a neighborhood in northwest Baltimore, on August 28, 1911, and was buried in New Orleans.

Rock, William C.: Not listed in Tennessee 1860 or 1870 census. Believed to be a gardener who worked at Belmont from December 1864 through May 1865. The *Nashville Union and Dispatch* on February 9, 1868, printed that he owed the city of Nashville $8.00 in taxes, which had accrued from 1857 to 1867.

Blair, William: Gardener at Belmont following the Civil War, most likely from May 1865 to May 1867. From May 1870 through May 1873, he worked as the gardener at the Tennessee Insane Asylum. Adelicia's third husband, Dr. William Cheatham, was the Tennessee Insane Asylum Medical Director prior to the Civil War.

William was also the gardener for P. L. Nichol. The *Nashville Union & American* on November 8, 1873, printed that in the preceding week a marriage license was issued for William Blair and Mary Sullivan. They moved to California around 1875. On February 12, 1878, the *Nashville Daily American* reported that Mrs. Mary Blair, wife of William Blair, formerly of Nashville, died in San Francisco. William was listed in the Oakland City Directory of 1881 and the San Francisco City Directory of 1882 as a nurseryman and gardener respectively.

Gray, Henry: Born ca. 1834, died 1916. He was a gardener, and was first mentioned in one of Adelicia's letters dated October 1868, as "getting his plants in before Frost." He was mentioned again in 1869, when Adelicia wrote that "the change of gardeners will be of great advantage because Mr. Gray has become unreliable." Because of the handwriting, it is difficult to know if Adelicia was referring to Mr. Gray or Mr. Geny, another Belmont gardener, but it was most likely Gray. It appears he went to work at the Tennessee Insane Asylum by July 1869. Adelicia's third husband, Dr. William Cheatham, was the Tennessee Asylum Medical Director prior to the Civil War.

Gray was elected a member of the newly reformed Tennessee Horticultural Society in April 1868 (*Nashville Union & Dispatch, February 9, 1868*). In the May 1868 issue of the *Gardener's Monthly* magazine, he was mentioned as the gardener at Belmont. In July 1869, he was working at the Tennessee Insane Asylum.

In January 1870, he was in partnership with William Heaver in the Edgefield Nursery while still working at the Asylum. That partnership dissolved on July 1, 1870 (*Nashville Union & American,* July 5, 1870), but he remained at the Asylum until he began to work for Mr. P. I. Nichol in October 1871. He was not found in the Davidson County Census of 1870, but was listed in the 1872 city directory living at 109 S. Cherry Street and working as a florist for P.L. Nichol, a florist and dealer in seeds, plants, and bulbs. The 1873 and 1874 directories listed Gray as a grocer, still living at 109 S. Cherry. In the 1875 directory, he was listed as a gardener working for Mr. Jacob McGavock and living at 320 Broadway. From 1876 onward, he cannot be found in a city directory.

The 1880 census listed Gray, age 44, living with wife Annie E., age 41; both were English-born. In January 1887, he was on the payroll of the Tennessee Insane Asylum as a florist at $55 per month. When records end for the Asylum on January 15, 1894, he was still employed.

The 1900 census listed Gray, age 64, who was born November 1835, and immigrated to the United States in 1861. He lived at the Asylum in Davidson County and was married to Annie, age 61, born in May 1839. He cannot be found in the 1910 census. He died on November 4, 1916, at age 82 and was buried at Mt. Olivet Cemetery (Section 13). Annie died at age 75 on July 3, 1914, and was also buried at Mt. Olivet.

According to family tradition, when Adelicia moved to Washington, D.C., she and Dr. Cheatham gave Mr. Gray prints of Queen Victoria and Prince Albert. The Grays later gave these prints to William K. Nicholson (who also worked at the Asylum). The prints are still in the possession of his descendants.

Luizard, Charles: (also spelled Louigard) Born in France ca. 1849-50. He worked as Adelicia's footman and possibly driver from 1866 to about 1870. He was listed on the ship's manifest as a servant, age 15 or 16, traveling with Adelicia when she returned from her Grand Tour in 1866, and was mentioned in a letter from Adelicia in October 1868.

Liveried servants on Adelicia's carriage were mentioned in the *Republican Banner* on October 10, 1866. In November that same year, Albigence Waldo Putnam, an elder at First Presbyterian Church, recalled seeing Adelicia arrive at church with a French driver on a carriage box wearing livery and a cockade.

The 1870 United States Census listed Luizard as a cook at the Maxwell House Hotel. On February 23, 1873, the *Republican Banner* printed a story about his train accident. After Adelicia brought him from France to be her footman, he went to work at the Maxwell House Hotel before eventually hiring on with the railroad. While working for the railroad, he fell from the train and broke his arm in several places. The arm was amputated and he died on February 25 at the age of 22 from complications following surgery. He was buried in an unmarked grave at Mount Olivet Cemetery. (Section 2, Lot 14, range 1)

Mullins, Mike: Born in Ireland in 1820 and immigrated to the United States in 1853. In 1854, he was living in Blair County, Pennsylvania. He made a declaration of intention to become a U.S. citizen at the 1854 October Term of the Court of Common Pleas in Blair County. The 1859 city directory listed him as a laborer at M. Jackson & Company, owned by Claiborne Machine Works.

There was no Michael Mullins listed in the 1860 census in Davidson County, nor in the 1860-1861 or 1865 city directories. On August 1, 1863, *Nashville Daily Union* reported he was the assistant gardener to Owen Sharkey at the Tennessee Insane Asylum. M. Mullins was listed as a laborer in the 1866 directory, but there was no listing from 1867 onward.

Adelicia first mentioned he was a workman in a letter dated October 1868. In April 1869, Adelicia wrote that "Mike [could be Mullins] and John are with us on the place and stays in the cottage [most likely the gardener's cottage behind the water tower.]." In the same letter, she also mentioned Gray or Geny (most likely Gray) was becoming unreliable as the gardener.

Mullins was listed in the 1870 census as living at Belmont as a common laborer, age 43. In 1880, he was listed as a gardener along with Valentine Fisher (see page 50). In May 1869, Owen Sharkey, to whom Mullins was an assistant at the asylum, was the gardener. In September 1873, Leon Geny became the gardener for one year. Other than Valentine Fisher in the 1880 census, there were no references to any other gardeners from this time forward.

Mullins became a citizen on June 28, 1878, in the Davidson County Court (Minute Book Q, page 613, mf roll 1620). He was listed in the 1880 census, age 51, single, gardener, living at Belmont. He appears to have worked at Belmont until it was sold in 1887.

The 1889 City Directory listed him as a gardener on Church Street at the corner of Boyd. In 1894, he boarded at 904 Kayne Avenue and worked as a florist. He cannot be found in the 1900 census. In 1901, he was at the same residence as in 1894, but his occupation was listed as gardener. He died at the age of 87 in Nashville on January 14, 1907, at 12:30 a.m. and was buried at Calvary Cemetery in an unmarked grave.

Amanda: Cook for Adelicia in October 1868. In April 1869, Adelicia wrote that she had a new cook but gave no name. This may be the same Amanda who was the daughter of Betsy, an enslaved woman given to Adelicia by her father O. B. Hayes in 1839. Listed in the September 1847 inventory of Isaac Franklin's estate and in an October 1857 legal document. She was possibly the same Amanda (with no last name given) who was buried in the Nashville City Cemetery on March 10, 1871.

Joshua: Mentioned as a servant in October 1868.

Delia: In letters written in October 1868, Adelicia referred to her as a servant. Known to have worked in the dining room as late as April 1869.

Liddy: Mentioned in October 1868 letter as the washerwoman. In April 1869, mentioned as being in the nursery and bedrooms.

Sharkey, Owen S.: Born 1824, died 1879. Received his training in Scotland and worked as a gardener in San Francisco before moving to Nashville. He cannot be found in the 1860 census records in Nashville. The July 9, 1863, *Nashville Daily Union* mentioned he was superintending the Horticultural Department at the Tennessee Insane Asylum. The same newspaper on August 1, 1863, listed Michael Mullins, later a Belmont gardener, as his assistant. In a paper given to the Pennsylvania Horticultural Society on March 3, 1868, he was listed as a gardener at the Tennessee Insane Asylum. A May 20, 1869, newspaper article listed him as a gardener at Belmont.

He appears to have worked at the asylum until he came to work at Belmont in 1869.

In the 1870 Census, he was listed as a U.S. citizen, born in Ireland, and living with the Lishley family, a local greenhouse grower. Newspaper accounts indicated he was back working at Belmont in October 1871 and remained there until he went to work at the Tennessee Insane Asylum in July 1873. Adelicia's third husband Dr. William Cheatham was the Asylum Medical Director before the Civil War and remained involved there until his death.

Following Sharkey's work at Belmont and the asylum, in 1876 he became the greenhouse keeper at Mt. Olivet Cemetery when the first greenhouse was built. According to newspaper reports, he was considered one of the top gardeners in Nashville. He died in
July 1879 in Shelbyville, Tennessee, while working as a gardener for Mr. J. D. Whilhoite. Sharkey was buried at Willow Mount Cemetery in Shelbyville. (*Find a Grave #92805763*)

## *1870s*

Buhla, Frederick: Listed in 1870 census, age 32. A common laborer born in Baden, Germany. He cannot be found beyond 1870.

Buhla, Josephine: Wife of Frederick. Listed in the 1870 census, age 24, and born in Switzerland. She was living at Belmont, but did not work for Adelicia. She cannot be found beyond 1870.

Fleming, Mary: Listed 1870 census as an African American servant, age 28. Born in Tennessee. This could possibly be Mary Ann, daughter of Maria, who was a slave given to Adelicia in 1839 by her father O. B. Hayes. If she were a year old or less, her actual age would have been 31 in 1870. (A three year age difference is within range-of-age discrepancies found in the census.)

The 1880 census also listed a Mary Fleming, widowed, age 45, living in Nashville with her son Alex Stoddard and his wife. The 1888 city directory listed a Mary Fleming, widow of John, living at 813 Church Street in Nashville.

The 1900 census listed a Mary Fleming, widowed, age 60. Born February 1840, she had two children with only one still living. She was a cook for the Noel family (who were related to the Acklens) and could not read nor write. It appears this was the same Mary Fleming who died three miles out Granny White Pike on September 17, 1906, at the age of 75 and was buried in Mount Ararat Cemetery. (Death Certificate V. 3, Record 486)

Golden, John: Worked as a teamster (driver of service wagons). Listed in 1870 census, living at Belmont, age 37. Born in Ireland. He was not in the 1860 Census in Nashville. Born in 1833, died on May 22, 1880, and was buried at Calvary Cemetery. (Section 12, Lot 28, Space 1)

Haley, Mildred: Listed in 1870 census as an African American seamstress, age 25. Born in Tennessee, and living at Belmont. She cannot be located in the census past 1870.

Horton, Sophia: Listed in 1870 census as a white servant, age 39. Born in Tennessee, and living at Belmont. She cannot be located past 1870.

Winkler, Elias: Listed in 1870 census as a gardener (most likely assistant to Owen Sharkey), age 27, born in Switzerland, U.S. citizen by 1870. Cannot be found in the 1860 census.

There was an Elias Winkler in the 1880 Adams County, Ohio Census, age 27, born in Switzerland, and working as a farmer.

His wife was Ann Eliza, age 20, from Ohio. He cannot be located past 1880 in the census records.

Winkler, John: Listed in 1870 census as a common laborer at Belmont, age 25, born in Switzerland; U.S. citizen.

There are too many John Winklers in the 1880 census of the correct approximate age, mainly in Illinois and Ohio, to determine who might have worked at Belmont.

Winstead, Margaret M.: Listed in 1870 census as a mulatto house servant, age 21. Born in Tennessee, and working at Belmont. She cannot be found beyond the 1870 census.

Young, John: Listed in 1870 census, as an African American footman, age 9. Born in Tennessee, and working at Belmont.

With such a common name, it was too difficult to determine the correct John Young from census records. There were numerous entries in the 1880 census and beyond that could match this former Belmont employee.

Acklen, Ella Mason: (1842/43-1913) Letters of Adelicia first mention her as a tutor in June of 1871. The last reference to her was in November of the same year when she accompanied the family to the plantations. Adelicia, in her will signed January 22, 1884, bequeathed "to my friend Miss Ella Mason" a set of amethyst jewelry.

Ella was the daughter of Julia Taylor and T. N. Mason of Macon, Georgia. In 1891, she married the Acklens' youngest son Claude in Ellicott City, Maryland, where they were both living at the time. It is believed she was teaching at the Patapsco Female Institute (1837-1891). Ella and Claude separated in 1905. She then moved to Nicholasville, Kentucky, where she taught at the Jessammine Female Institute until a few years before her death. On December 16, 1913, Ella died at the home of her niece in Nicholasville. Her body was returned to Macon, Georgia, for burial in Rose Hill Cemetery. (Lot 16, Block 8. Section; Central Ave. Division)

## *1880s*

Buford, Nellie (could also be Mollie): Listed in the 1880 census as an African American housekeeper, age 21. Born in Tennessee. She had a son, Frank, who was one year old at the time of the census. She cannot be located past 1880.

A Mollie Buford died on May 7, 1890, at the age of 40. She was born in Tennessee, widowed and living at 323 Russell Street when she died of heart disease. She was buried at Rest Home Cemetery (location unknown). (Death Certificate # 279)

Cheatham, Armstead: Listed in 1880 census as an African American coachman, age 35. Born in Tennessee (this would make his birthdate ca. 1845), and living at Belmont. Because the 1883 city directory listed him residing on Hamilton Street at the corner of Watkins, he apparently had stopped working at Belmont sometime before 1883. According to tradition, he purchased Adelicia's carriage at the estate sale and still had the carriage at the time of his death.

He was the son of Callie Neal and Anderson Cheatham (Death Certificate #D1613). He married Fannie Watkins on October 28, 1886, presided by Reverend J.M. Gilmere/Gilmore. In the same year, he moved to 61 North Margin Street. The 1888 city directory listed him as a driver at 175 North Market, with a corresponding residential address of 304 Morgan. He was listed at the same home address in 1889. In the 1890 and 1891 directories, he was listed as a sick nurse with the same address on Morgan Street.

The 1900 census recorded his age as 45, born in March 1855. At the time of the census, he had been married for 13 years, and worked as a porter. He could read and write, and owned his house. He lived with his wife Fannie, age 49, born August 1850; she could not read or write. Alice Watkins, age 7, lived in the house, as well.

The 1904 city directory listed him as a porter, still on Morgan Street. The 1909 directory listed him as an expressman living at the same address. The 1910 census listed his age as 50, married 22 years, and living with his wife, Fannie, age 63, now able to read but not write. The 1910 and 1914 city directories recorded him as an expressman, living at 304 13$^{th}$ Avenue North. In the 1915 directory, he was at the same 13$^{th}$ Avenue address, but was working as a driver for Warner Drug Co.

By the 1920 census, he was listed as age 60, living with Fannie, age 65, owning their own home, but without an occupation. The 1922 city directory recorded him as a porter, still living at 304 13$^{th}$ Avenue North. He died at his home on March 26, 1923, at the age of 75, survived by his wife Fannie. He was buried at Mt. Ararat Cemetery. (*Nashville Banner March 27, 1923,* page 18)

Fisher (Fischer), Valentine: Immigrated to United States in 1857, but not found in the 1860 census. Listed in 1870 census as born March 30, 1837 (his tombstone records 1833), in the German province of Hesse-Darmstadt. He worked as a carpenter and lived in Nashville with the Prussian Schoupfley family of bee-keepers and gardeners. Listed in 1880 census as living at Belmont, age 42, single, gardener. Made declaration to become a U.S. citizen on July 20, 1885, at the July term in the County Court of Davidson County (page 181, Book V; mf roll 1622 and 1623, Tennessee State Library and Archives), He became a U.S. citizen on August 18, 1887. The 1892 city directory listed him as a florist, living on Patterson at the corner of Boyd. In the 1893 directory, the address was the same, but he was listed as a gardener. In 1896 and 1899, the directory recorded him as a gardener, with a corresponding business address of Church at the corner of Boyd. The 1900 directory listed him as a gardener, with the same business address as 1896 and 1899, living on Patterson at the corner of Boyd. The 1900 census listed him as a retired florist living at a hotel in Nashville. He was recorded as being able to read, write, and speak English.

He died in Nashville on November 7, 1900, at the Commerce Hotel and was buried at Mt. Olivet Cemetery (sec. 10, lot #446), with services by the Aurora Lodge of I.O.O.F. on November 9, 1900. (Death Certificate #D1613). His will was signed on the day of his death and made provisions for the purchase of a tombstone. He left money to nieces and nephews living in Baltimore, children of two of his brothers. He also left money to a deceased brother's (Andrew) children who were living in Germany. (Original will in Metro Archives. Probate 11/10/1900. *Will book 35,* page 479. *Minute Books S: 578.*)

Sittell, Agnes: Listed in the 1880 census as a white housekeeper, age 39. Born in Scotland, divorced, and living at Belmont.

Robertson, William: Adelicia's carriage driver. In Adelicia's will, signed on January 22, 1884, she bequeathed to "carriage driver Wm. Robertson $200 to be placed in the bank and drawn out ¼ at a time annually." There were several people named William Robertson in the Nashville City Directories starting in 1886.

*NOTE: THE FOLLOWING INFORMATION IS TAKEN FROM BOARD OF ASSESSIONS RECORDS WHEN ADELICIA ACKLEN WAS APPLYING FOR DAMAGES DONE BY THE UNION ARMY WHILE OCCUPYING THE BELMONT MANSION PROPERTY BEFORE AND DURING THE BATTLE OF NASHVILLE.*

## BOARD OF ASSESSIONS RECORDS

Nashville, Tennessee, August 2, 1865

Proceedings of Board of Assessions in the case of Mrs. A. Acklin [sic.] The Board then proceeded to take evidence in the case of Mrs. A. Acklin [sic] as to destruction of property as set forth in the following bill viz. [Note Acklen is spelled *Acklin* throughout this document.]

### The United States
### To Mrs. A. Acklin Dr.

| No. | Items | Dollars |
|---|---|---|
| 1 | 1 Brick Dwelling House Tin Roof | 3,000 |
| 2 | 4 "     "     "     "     " | 10,000 |
| 3 | 1 Stable and Corn Crib | 300 |
| 4 | 1 Barn and Shed | 1,200 |
| 5 | 1 Smoke House | 200 |
| 6 | 1 Turkey House | 50 |
| 7 | 1 Poultry House | 150 |
| 8 | 3,000 yards Stone fence damaged & destroy | 2,700 |
| 9 | 400    " Plank fence and posts | 500 |
| 10 | 2,000   " Picket fence | 1,500 |
| 11 | Damage to Cisterns and pumps | 80 |
| 12 | 2 large Gates and Posts | 40 |
| 13 | 32 Sheep | 64 |
| 14 | 7 Milch [sic] Cows | 280 |
| 15 | 5 Beef Cattle | 375 |
| 16 | 4 Calves | 20 |
| 17 | 6 Goats | 25 |
| 18 | 2 Mules | 225 |
| 19 | 3 Horses | 300 |
| 20 | 150 Poultry | 45 |
| 21 | Stock Hogs | 375 |
| | **Total** | **$21,577** |

Judge Nathaniel Baxter being duly Sworn testifies as follows: Should think there was 3,500 yards (as described in Item 8) of Stone fence thrown down, considerable [sic] being put into the line of works by the U.S. Forces. - I have engaged to have a stone fence put up at one dollar per yard provided the Stone can be quarried within one-hundred yards, without blasting. Think that $2,700 for rebuilding the 3,500 yards would be full compensation there being an average of one foot of the fence standing. Think the gate on Hillsboro Pike (as described in item 12) would cost $20 to replace I know nothing of the other gate. Think a flock of sheep would be worth $2.00 per head.

William C. Rock being duly Sworn testifies as follows: Am in the employ of Mrs. Acklin as gardner [sic]. I know of one 2 story brick dwelling House and 3 or 4 one story brick dwelling houses, one log Stable, one picket post barn and one Shed. Know nothing of Smoke house, Turkey House and Poultry House. - There were about two miles of stone fence. Some was used in the Breastworks and the balance [sic] is lying about on the ground - there was about 400 yards of Plank fence (in the rear of family dwelling) burnt up. There was about 1,800 or 2,000 yards of picket fencing 5 feet high taken, part was used in the Breastworks and part burnt up. - Know of no damage done to Cisterns. Some of the pumps were broken in use by the Soldiers - two large gates were broken and burnt up. - Know nothing about Sheep or Milch [sic] cows. 2 beef Cattle were taken while I was there. Know nothing of Calves, Goats, Mules, Horses, Poultry or stock Hogs taken. -

The 2 Story brick Dwelling and the 3 or 4 one Story Negro quarters were torn down Part of the Brick were used in the Breastworks, The Balance [sic], except the pieces, were Sold by Mrs. Acklin to Messrs McCune and Leonard at $10.00 per thousand/ do not know how many were sold. The articles that I have mentioned as being taken or destroyed, was done by the 4th army Corps Genl Wood commanding with Hdqtrs at Mrs Acklin's house.

Fredrick Kipp. Musician 10 Michigan Inftry. Vols. being duly sworn testifies as follows: I have been detailed as safe guard at the Acklin farm. went there Sept 30th 1864. The 2 story brick dwelling house was a good substantial house. It was hauled down by Genl. Wood's division of the 4th Corps and used in the Breastworks. There was only 3 one story brick dwellings that I know of. They were also hauled down by Genl Wood's Division of the 4th Corps and used in the Breastworks. 1 Stable and corn Crib, 1 barn and Shed, 1 Smoke house, 1 Turkey house and 1 Poultry house were taken down by Genl Wood's Division of the 4th Corp and used in the Breastworks, for firewood and other purposes. - I should think there was all of 3,500 yards of Stone fence about 4 feet high. of some was taken down and used in the Breastworks and Soldier's cabins by Genl Woods Division of the 4th Corp. I should think there was 400 of Plank fence and posts and 2,000 yards of Picket fence carried away by Wood's Division of the 4th Corps for firewood, there were two Cisterns and two pumps. the pumps were broken by the Soldiers of Genl Woods Division And were then obliged to take the tops of the Cisterns off to procure water and in so doing the walls caved in. - The 2 large gates and posts situated on the Granny White and Hillsboro Pikes, were used for firewood by the teamsters of Genl Woods Division train I know nothing of 23 Sheep - Two Milch [sic] cows one 3 year old Bull, four yearling Heifers and 2 Calves (6 weeks old) were taken by Genl Woods Division of the 4th Army Corps. I know nothing of 6 goats 2 mules 3 Horses and 150 poultry. - one Sow and two young pigs were taken by the Soldiers of Genl Woods Division of the 4th Army Corps.

    Mrs. Acklin Sold (40,000) forty thousand brick at $10.00 per thousand. The Bricks in breastwork can be taken out and used again. The stone from the fence is nearby and can be used again in the fence. The Barn was made of Picket Posts of Cedar and was about 24 by 48 feet. The Shed was of Plank with tine [sic] roof and was about 16 by 30 feet. - The foundations of the brick houses are still there, they are Stone.

The Stable and corn crib were of plank with tin roof. The smoke house Turkey and Poultry houses were of Brick. The turkey house was two Stories. The others only one story with tin roofs. They were six or eight cornered, they were 8 or 10 feet high. I know nothing about the value of any of this property.

  William L. B. Lawrence being duly Sworn testifies as follows: - I live adjoining Mrs. A. Acklin's place, Know that a 2 story and 3 one storied brick buildings belonging to Mrs. A Acklin were torn down by Genl Woods Corp of U.S. Forces and used in the Breastworks. A Stable and Corn Crib and one Barn and Shed were used the same was. I do not recollect [sic] the other outbuildings. Mr. Shields and Mrs. Acklin desired me to make an estimate of the fencings. Mr. Shields was with me. We concluded there was about 3,500 yards of Stone fence down and damaged. The larger portion of it was scattered about, there was 300 or 400 yards of plank fence in rear of family residence entirely destroyed, it was about 5 feet high. There was about 200 yards of picket fence South of Mrs. Acklins between her and my lot destroyed it was about 4 1/2 feet high. it was orriginaly [sic] put up at her expence [sic]. I have repaired it and Sometimes She has. Know nothing of damage to Cistern and pumps. Know of two large gates and posts destroyed.

  This property was taken or destroyed by genl Woods Corp of U.S. Forces about the middle of December 1864. Do not know that they took any Sheep, Calves, Goats, Mules, Cows, Horses, Poultry or Hogs from Mrs. Acklin. - Should think the 2 story building was worth $3,000.00 and the 3 one storied quarters about $1,000.00 each. - the Stables and corn crib was worth about $1,500.00. Should think from present prices of labor that it would be worth 90 cents per yard. A part of the stone fence with the stone lying about and in Breastworks as they are now. - Should think it would be worth $3,600 to replace the board fence with Cedar posts it was worth 45 cts per yard. - think it worth double now. The picket fence was made of Cedar rails sawed in two. Cedar rails are worth $5.00 per hundred. think one hundred rails would make one hundred feet of fence. Digging trenchs [sic] and putting up would be worth about $5.00 per hundred feet. Total cost would be about $10.00 per hundred feet.

The large gates and posts were worth about $10.00 each. - Mrs Acklin owned this property in her own right before marraige[sic]. - I am Mrs Acklin's Brother-in-law. Mr. Acklin was not worth anything to the best of my knowledge. - I know there was a company raised in Nashville for the Rebel Service in 1861 called the "Acklin Rifles." Do not know of Mrs Acklins Equiping [sic] this or any other company. Mr. Acklin told me he had given the Capt. of the company one hundred dollars to use for the company benefit.

George W. Shields, merchant, and agent for Mrs. Acklin being duly sworn testifies: Know that a 2 Story brick dwelling, three one Story brick & what I supposed was another brick but have since learned was a one Story frame. - Was on Mrs. Acklin's farm, and were destroyed by U.S. Forces in December. - Know there was several outbuildings, but do not recollect [sic] character of them. Mr. Lawrance [sic] and myself estimated that there was 3,500 yards Stone fence partly down, the stone are near the fortifications and about where the tents were. - The plank fence was estimated at 400 yards. This was entirely destroyed. - 2,000 yards of picket fence was also estimated same time. The Cisterns and pumps were in good order before genl. Woods went there, and were damaged when he left, 2 gates were damaged same time. Know that Mrs. Acklin had some stock before Genl. Woods Corps occupied the place and that there was not as much when he went away. - Do not know value of property damaged or destroyed. Know Mr Acklin, Husband of Mrs. Acklin, Do not think he was worth anything except what he was entitled to for the management of Mrs Acklin's property in Louisiana. I rented on November last to Mr. A. R. Goodwin the 2 Story brick dwelling and four

Smaller ones with all outbuildings with the gardens and twenty or thirty acres of pasturing for his own stock for six hundred dollars a year. He was to have had possession January 1st 1865. the buildings and fences being destroyed he did not take it. -

 Thomas Bowstead, farmer, being duly Sworn testifies as follows- I live adjoining Mrs. Acklins farm. there were 5 Houses destroyed, 4 were brick and one frame; there was 1 Stable & Corn Crib destroyed it was large and could hold 10 Horses. - I don't know of Barn & Shed Smoke house, Turkey and Poultry houses being destroyed. Should suppose there was about 3,000 yards of Stone fence destroyed.- have never examined same - Know nothing of Company called the "Acklin Rifles," except by hearsay - Know that Mrs Acklin had some stock, but do not know that any of it was taken. I know nothing of any other items in Mrs. Acklin's bill than those I have mentioned. I don't know who destroyed these buildings nor the probable cost of repairing or replacing them. I do not know whether the fence or buildings were destroyed before or after Hood came near Nashville or if said property was destroyed by U.S. Forces. -

 William Acklin, Colored, being duly sworn testifies as follows. - I have been in the employ of Mrs. Acklin for the past 19 years. I know of there being one brick dwelling house 2 Storics high with tin roof but cannot state value. Know of there being 4 Brick dwelling Houses with two rooms each, one story high. Know of all the houses being torn down and used in the breastworks and Fortifications by the U.S. Forces.

 I know of there being a frame Stable and corn crib which were torn down but can't state dimentions [sic] or what it was used for. one Barn and Shed, one Smoke house, one Turkey and one Poultry house were all torn down but can't state what they were used for. I should think there was 3,500 yards of Stone fence about four feet high which was taken by U.S. Forces for the construction of the fortifications. But can't state what command they belonged too [sic].

There were 400 yards of plank fence and posts, and 200 yards of Picket fence carried away, But can't state who by. There were three cisterns and three wells. They were all damaged the Stocks [?] were all broken off by the Soldiers. Know of their large gates and posts all of which were capped. they were all torn down and destroyed while the place was occupied by the U.S. Forces But cant State who by - I know of there being on the place 232 Sheep 7 Milch [sic] Cows 5 Beef Cattle 2 Calves 6 Goats 2 Mules 8 Horses 150 poultry 35 Stock hogs, taken from the place while the grounds were occupied by the U.S. troops but can't say who they were taken by.

James C. Terry Citizen, being duly Sworn testifies as follows. I was living on Mrs. Acklins place at the time the lines were formed on the place by the U.S. and rebels in December 1864. I was living in the overseer's house. The one called a two Story, but it was only a Story and a half.

The U.S. line of works ran over where this house stood. I left the house some eight or ten days before the fight. There were three other brick houses one story and two frame houses all torn down and used in different ways, principaly [sic] in building chimneys for tents. The frame houses were used in the breast works. Barn Stable corn crib Shed and Cribs were all torn down by the U.S. Forces frame Smoke house, Small, say 12 by 14 [ft]. Turkey house, frame, good size, And Poultry house, frame, good size, were also destroyed. There was a good deal of stone fence and some Picket fencing torn down. one pump was broken but do not know how bad. Four Gates and posts were destroyed. Know nothing of any Sheep. Know nothing of any Cows Calves Cattle Goats Mules Horses chickens or hogs being taken by U.S. Forces from Mrs. Acklin. Think the large brick house worth about $2,500 think the other three brick houses worth about $2,000 each. Frame worth nothing except for lumber, think it worth about $75.00 small frame worth about the same. Stable, Corn Crib, Barn and Shed were worth altogether about $1,500 Smoke house worth about

$40.00 Turkey house and Poultry house worth about $100.00 each Think as the stone is lying about and in Breastworks near the line of fence that the Stone fence could be put up in as good condition as it was before for one dollar per yard. It would be worth about $300 to replace the Cedar Picket fence.

The four gates and posts could be replaced for about $20.00 each. It was the common report in town and country that Mrs. Acklin had equipped a Rebel Company called the "Acklin Guards" I was living at that time within two miles of Nashville and within one mile of Mrs. Acklins place. Since the Federal Army came here She has been reported a Union woman, never knew her to do anything that led me to believe she was a Union woman. I lived on her place nearly two years.

In the above case of Mrs. A. Acklin we find that the property mentioned below was taken by, and for the use of the United States and have assessed the damages as set opposite the items:

| Item | Dollars |
|---|---|
| Large Brick House | 2,622.50 |
| 3 Small " " @ $1,000.00 | 3,000 |
| Frame " " | 150 |
| Stable Barn Shed and Crib | 1,200 |
| Smoke House | 40 |
| Turkey " | 100 |
| Poultry " | 100 |
| 3,500 Yards Stone fence | 2,465.50 |
| Plant fence and posts | 360 |
| Picket fence | 5,220 |
| 2 Large Gates and posts | 25 |
| 2 Cows | 75 |
| 4 Heifers and 1 Bull | 120 |
| 2 Calves | 20 |
| 1 Sow and 2 Pigs | 20 |
| **Total** | **$10,817** |

From this amount [sic] deduct 40,000
Brick Sold by Mrs Acklin @40 per
[?] $400
Estimated value of good brick in
Earthworks $1,000                                    1,400
                                    **Total  $9,417**

    The Damage to Cisterns and pumps was trifling in value. The Sheep, Goats, Mules Horses, Poultry and Stock Hogs were mentioned by but one witness and he did not know who took them. But two cows proved to have been taken by the U.S. Forces.

    From the testimony we believe Mrs. A. Acklin and her husband, during his lifetime, to have been not only disloyal, but notoriously so. A company for the Rebel Army was raised here and in honor of the family was called the "Acklin [sic] Guards, or Rifles".

    For this reason we would recommend that no part of the assessed damages be paid.

    Respectfully Submitted

    J. C. Frankeberger
    Lt Col 188th Ohio Inft & Pss [?] Board

    U. J. Vail
    Major 14th US Inftry

    W. Stoey
    1st Lieut 78th ??? [unreadable]

    H. A. Baker
    1st G 100 o.o.d.
    and Recorder

Office Board of Assessions
Nashville Tenn Aug 2nd 1865

Major H. M. Cist

AA Genl

Sir, In accordance with instructions of Aug 1st received this day this Board has closed the only unfinished case now before them. You will find Lew with the case of Mrs. A. Acklin with our award, also the papers refered to the Board but which have not yet been commenced by thomas Gale and W.B. Evans Ms Sarah A. Gordon and Ms Mary L. Clements the latter one was this day received.
      All cases now before the Board are closed out or herewith returned

I am very Respectfully

## SLAVE SCHDEULE, U. S. CENSUS, 1860
## ENSLAVED PEOPLE AT BELMONT

| Age | Gender | Race |
|---|---|---|
| 45 | Female | Mulatto |
| 30 | Female | Black |
| 30 | Male | Black |
| 30 | Male | Black |
| 25 | Female | Mulatto |
| 25 | Female | Black |
| 25 | Male | Black |
| 25 | Male | Black |
| 24 | Female | Mulatto |
| 24 | Male | Black |
| 22 | Female | Black |
| 22 | Male | Mulatto |
| 20 | Female | Black |
| 20 | Male | Black |
| 20 | Male | Black |
| 18 | Female | Mulatto |
| 18 | Male | Black |
| 18 | Male | Black |
| 16 | Female | Black |
| 15 | Female | Black |
| 13 | Male | Black |
| 12 | Male | Black |
| 11 | Male | Black |
| 10 | Female | Mulatto |
| 8 | Female | Black |
| 6 | Female | Black |
| 5 | Male | Black |
| 4 | Male | Black |
| 3 | Male | Black |
| 3 | Male | Black |
| 2 | Male | Black |
| 1 | Female | Black |

**ENSLAVED PEOPLE STATISTICS**
Enslaved people  Age Range: 1-45
Number of Males: 18
Number of Females: 14
10 Male adults
10 Female adults
12 under the age of 15
Total Number of Slave at West Feliciana and  Belmont: 691 (32 at Belmont)

# UNITED STATES AGRICULTURAL CENSUS, 1860

<u>LIVESTOCK</u>
Horses: 14
Mules: 6
Milk Cows: 6
Other Cattle: 15
Sheep: 20
Swine: 15
Value of Livestock: $5,650

Bushels of Indian Corn: 500
Bushels of Oats: 300
Wool: 40 (?)
Bushels of Irish Potatoes: 75
Bushels of Sweet Potatoes: 75
Pounds of Butter: 350
Tons of Hay: 40


<u>MONTVALE FARM</u>
Turkey House
Poultry House
Stable and corn crib
Barn with shed
Smokehouse
Overseer's House

www.ingramcontent.com/pod-product-compliance
Lightning Source LLC
Chambersburg PA
CBHW051958290426
44110CB00015B/2294